AIN'T GONNA LET NOBODY TURN ME 'ROUND

AIN'T GONNA LET NOBODY TURN ME 'ROUND

My Story of the Making of
Martin Luther King Day

KATHLYN J. KIRKWOOD

ILLUSTRATED BY
STEFFI WALTHALL

Versify • *An Imprint of HarperCollinsPublishers* • Boston • New York

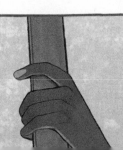

In memory of my mom and dad,
Mrs. Texana and Mr. Mack C. Wiggins,
who led by example—who showed me how to be

For all the nameless and faceless foot soldiers
past, present, and future

The Library of Congress Cataloging-in-Publication Data has been applied for.

ISBN: 978-0-358-38726-8

The text was set in Garamond Premier Pro.

"How a Bill Becomes a Law" infographic by Chenjelani Whatley

Cover design by Whitney Leader-Picone and Camryn Cogshell

Interior design by Chelsea Hunter

Manufactured in the United States of America

1 2021

4500841006

First Edition

We ain't going back, we've come too far, marched too long, prayed too hard, wept too bitterly, bled too profusely, and died too young to let anybody turn back the clock on our journey for justice.

—REVEREND JOSEPH LOWERY,
Dean of the Civil Rights Movement

FOREWORD

....

For so many of us, so much of the past is a vague memory.
A dry paragraph in a history book about some people somewhere
marching. Dr. Martin Luther King Jr.—a mountaintop speech—
if that's remembered. Or more often, a holiday. Selma—a movie.
Jim Crow—a thing that happened to some people somewhere
a long time ago. Once, while doing a school visit, a fifth-grader
asked me if I had been born a slave. And other questions from
the mouths of otherwise brilliant young people—*What's a
Ku Klux Klan?* and *I think Moses burned a cross on the
mountaintop* and *How come Black people are still so mad?
They got equality already.*

When we forget our past, it's hard to understand our present.
Harder still to imagine our future. *Ain't Gonna Let Nobody
Turn Me 'Round* is a love song to the past by someone who was
there. Kathlyn Kirkwood tells her story with warmth, love, and
keen memory.

The past wasn't always pretty. It wasn't always kind. It was
never easy. But it is the shoulders we stand on now. As we
continue to fight toward a world where all people have the

same civil rights, we can open this book, dive into the narrative in verse, and step into a movement that would forever change America. We can meet the people who were a part of that movement. We can grow to love them and begin to understand our connection not only to the past, but to the people who resisted and fought for the rights we have today.

Ain't Gonna Let Nobody Turn Me 'Round—a title coming from the African American civil rights song from the early twentieth century—is just as relevant now as it was then. We are on a journey toward something better. And we really aren't letting anyone stop us.

While the people who were there still live and are able to tell their stories of the past, we must lean in and listen. And through the listening, remember.

—JACQUELINE WOODSON

AIN'T GONNA LET NOBODY TURN ME 'ROUND

. . . .

You don't know my face or my name,
but the day Dr. Martin Luther King Jr. was killed,
I became a **foot soldier:**

a doer, a worker, an everyday activist
in the Civil Rights Movement.

1968

I was just seventeen,
a senior at Booker T. Washington High
in Memphis, Tennessee.
I was editor in chief of our yearbook,
The Warrior,
and I played clarinet in the marching band.
Yay for the green and gold!

Kathlyn and her
brother Mack Carlos
in band uniform,
getting ready to
start stepping high.

The Cotton Makers Jubilee parade was the Black community's annual celebration of the cotton harvest on Beale Street, separate from the Whites-only Cotton Carnival celebrated on Main Street.

We loved stepping high
to the musical beats
led by the
crowd-pleasing
majorettes and drum major,
erect and tall,
right down Beale Street
in the Cotton Makers Jubilee parade,
the **colored** folks' celebration of
the cotton industry.

We couldn't go to the
"Whites only" Cotton Carnival
to see the king and queen's grand arrival
as they stepped off the royal barge
on the Mississippi River
into their royal carriage,
followed by lavishly decorated,
ornate floats pulled
by colored men.

WHILE WE STEPPED

· ·

Ugly things were happening in America,
especially in the Deep South.
Jim Crow was the law—
racism, discrimination,
and segregation of Blacks and Whites.

Made a lot of Black folks mad.

I was just seventeen
but it made me mad too.

One man was leading the fight for change:
Dr. Martin Luther King Jr.
Preacher, teacher, drum major for peace,
he led
    the Montgomery Bus Boycott
in Montgomery, Alabama,
    the Birmingham Campaign
in Birmingham, Alabama,

    the Freedom Walk
in Detroit, Michigan,
    and so many other demonstrations, prayer vigils,
    and nonviolent protests
for **freedom,**
for **justice,**
for **equality.**

Made a lot of White folks mad.

FEBRUARY 12, 1968

· ·

The Negro Memphis sanitation workers
went on strike.
They were **tired** of being treated like boys
instead of
men.

They did grueling work every day
with no place to eat,
no place to shower,
no sick days,
no vacation days,
no health care,
no pension plan,
for $1.70 an hour.

Some still needed welfare
just to live.

The Negro sanitation workers were just
BONE-TIRED.

HAVE YOU ST... ...AKING
The Commercial Appeal
AND
The Memphis Press-Scimitar?
WHY NOT?

1. They give unfair coverage to our Sanitation Workers!
2. They do not give fair and full coverage to Negro news!
3. They designate race when crimes are committed by Negroes, but not whites!
4. They insult us with "HAMBONE!"
5. They promote segregated housing through segregated classified ads!
6. They will not hire Negroes in most offices or departments!
7. They even segregate Negroes in death notices!

Stop being a traitor to the Negro's fight for freedom!
Start supporting the Sanitation Workers now!
Stop taking both the Commercial Appeal and Memphis Press-Scimitar!

Community On the Move for Equality
280 Hernando Street

The Community on the Move for Equality, a Memphis organization aimed at promoting social justice, called for boycotting the local newspapers because of their lack of support for the sanitation workers' strike and racist coverage of Negro news in general (i.e., *Hambone's Meditations* cartoons).

The National Guard was called in during the sanitation workers' strike in Memphis.

One day, as the men carried
leaky, maggot-filled garbage tubs
to the truck,
a packer blade malfunctioned.
Two men,
Echol Cole and Robert Walker,
were crushed to death.

The Negro sanitation workers
decided to fight
these horrible, inhumane working conditions.

They started marching
on Main Street **EVERY DAY.**
They wanted good pay, job safety,
and union recognition,
just like the White sanitation workers.

Seemed like NOBODY was listening.
But **Dr. King** was.

He halted his plans for the Poor People's Campaign
in Washington, DC, that would demand
Congress work to end poverty across America.
INSTEAD he came to Memphis
to support and lead a march for the sanitation workers.

MARCH 18, 1968

· ·

At my daddy's barbershop,
the men usually joked, laughed, shouted,
and told tall tales.

Not today.

The only thing they talked about was
why they were gonna march,
why they *had* to march.
Everyone remembered the two men who'd died,
the unfair pay, and how badly the
Negro sanitation workers were treated.

Flyers were everywhere.

Mr. Wiggins, Kathlyn's dad, cutting and styling, while waiting customers talk about supporting the striking sanitation workers and the upcoming protest march.

My friends and I were young,
but we wanted to march too.
I rushed home to see if I could.

Stone-faced, Mama said,
"Okay . . . but you have to stay close to Daddy."
I squealed and ran to call my friends.
"Mama said yes!"

All night,
I tossed and turned,
heart racing,
thinking,
imagining . . .

my first march.

Dr. Martin Luther King, Jr.
and

Community On the Move for Equality

INVITE YOU

To March for Justice and Jobs

FRIDAY, MARCH 22, 1968

9:00 A.M.
From Clayborn Temple A.M.E. Church
280 Hernando

We ask you to stay away from work or school and walk with more than 10,000 people who want Memphis once and for all to learn that it must be a city for all people. A man is a man. God requires that a man be treated like a man.

Memphis must do so in work, play, education, housing, by the police and in all other ways the rights of each man must be upheld. This will be a march of dignity. The only force we will use is soul-force which is peaceful, loving, courageous, yet militant.

MARCH INSTRUCTIONS:

1. Come to the church from Vance Street only.
2. THE ROUTE: Hernando to Beale
   To Main
   To Poplar
   To Second
   To Beale
   To Hernando
   To Clayborn Temple where we will disperse

3. Be ready to follow the instructions of the March Marshalls who will wear yellow arm bands.
4. We will march in the street.
5. Each organization can prepare a banner, no bigger than 6'x3' attached to at least two poles, which can carry the sign up above the heads of the marchers.

6. Walk gently, do not crowd those in front, when those stop you stop.

The Community on the Move for Equality spearheaded a march for justice.
Due to an ice storm, the protest march was rescheduled for March 28, 1968.

Have Sanitation Workers A Future?

Yes, If You Will Help To Build It!

How? That's Simple—

WE NEED YOU!

1. Do not shop downtown, or with the downtown branch stores anywhere in the city or any enterprise named Loeb.

2. Stop your subscriptions to the daily newspapers. Get news about the Movement from the radio or television or by joining the mass meetings. Be sure to pay your newspaper carrier his commission.

3. Do not buy new things for Easter. Let our Lent be one of sacrifices. What better way to remember Jesus' work for us and the world?

4. Support the workers with letters and telegrams to the Mayor and the City Council.

5. Join us in the daily marches downtown.

6. Call others each day and remind them of the movement.

7. Attend the nightly mass meetings Monday through Friday.

8. Do not place your garbage at the curb. Handle it the best way you can without helping the city and the Mayor's effort to break the strike.

9. Whenever you associate with white people, let them know what the issues are and why you support this cause.

10. Support the relief efforts for the workers and their families with gifts of money and food. Checks can be made out to "C.O.M.E." and food taken to Clayborn Temple A.M.E. Church, 280 Hernando.

- -

Community On the Move for Equality
WORK CARD

Name _____ Phone _____
Address _____
I will march _____   I will picket _____
I can answer phone or do clerical work _____
I can serve on a committee:
      Work Committee
      Telephone Committee _____
      Transportation Committee _____
Hours I can best serve:
  9:00am-11:00am _____   11:00am- 1:00pm _____
  1:00pm- 3:00pm _____   3:00pm- 6:00pm _____
  6:00pm- 8:00pm _____   8:00pm-10:00pm _____
  10:00pm-12:00pm _____

MARCH 28, 1968

. . . .

A perfect day,
cool but sunny.
My friends and I met at school
for homeroom roll call.
Then we skipped out
for the rest of the day
and joined about
twenty-two thousand
other students
from across the city
and a few teachers too.

Bubbling with anticipation,
my friends and I
rushed to meet my daddy
at his barbershop.
We couldn't sit still,
waiting for the marchers
to pass.

We stretched and strained
to see Dr. King
but the crowd was just too big.

Then we joined the march,
my daddy and me,
our friends,
and so many other
men, women, and children,
along the way.

Some, like my daddy, carried signs.
Somebody shouted, "What do we want?"

We shouted, "FREEDOM."
"When do we want it?"
I shouted, "NOW!"

We marched up Beale Street,
headed to Main Street.

This wasn't like
Mardi Gras or
the Cotton Makers Jubilee parade.

High school students from various Memphis city schools, including Kathlyn's classmates Janice Jones and Cassandra Hunt, singing and shouting "We shall overcome, and keep the faith, baby!" to support strikers who were being arrested for picketing businesses on Main Street, March 5, 1968.

This was a PROTEST march.

People came from all over the city,
energized, focused, and serious,
with one purpose:
JUSTICE for the Negro sanitation workers.

With each step,
I grew prouder and
more confident.

I felt like I was making a BIG difference.
I heard somebody say,
"There is power in numbers."

Suddenly,
shots rang out past our heads—
from where?

Not sure!

Then, breaking glass
and shattering windows.

It was an attack on the peaceful protesters,
my friends,
my dad,
and me.

Strikers scattered for safety when the march turned into a riot on March 28, 1968.

OUTSIDE AGITATORS CAUSED A RIOT

The marchers scattered,
scared and confused.
I lost my daddy and friends.
Dr. King was rushed away.

The police charged with
mace, tear gas, and nightsticks.

I thought that I was going to die.
Heart racing this time from FEAR,
I froze in place.

And then, just as suddenly,
I started to MOVE.
Running fast and hard,
heading for safety;
I ran toward HOME.

Almost there, just a few more blocks . . .
Turning the corner . . .
I saw my house on Kendale Avenue.
Joy and relief.
Home at last.

Mama didn't know about the riot.
Lines of worry invaded her face
as I relived how we'd marched peacefully—
until it turned into chaos and violence
without warning.

She rushed to call my daddy at the barbershop.
No answer.
She called again
and again.
Finally, he answered.
He was safe too.

But the riot
left one teen dead,
another sixty injured,
and two hundred and eighty arrested.

The looting and burning was bad.
It would cost a lot to make things
right again—

Well,
to fix the buildings and other stuff,
about—four hundred thousand dollars.
But no amount of money could fix
our hearts and minds.

Made us sad.
Made us mad.

Now, Memphis, Tennessee, was under a seven p.m. curfew.
And four thousand National Guardsmen
were on the way
to curb the chaos—
    the firebombs,
    the trash fires,
    the vandalism,
and looting of stores and businesses
mostly in the Negro neighborhoods . . .

to stop the

RIOT.

APRIL 3, 1968

Martin Luther King Jr. returns to Memphis to march again on April 3, 1968, with his aides Andrew Young, Ralph Abernathy, and Bernard Lee.

Undeterred, Dr. Martin Luther King Jr.
returned to Memphis
to march again.

That night,
my daddy,
a whole lot of
sanitation workers,
people from different neighborhoods,
local ministers, White union members,
and some White liberals too,
students—
both high-school and college-age—
filled up Mason Temple
to hear Dr. King.

Outside, the wind blew;
the rain was torrential;
the thunder and lightning crashed.
It felt like the world
was coming to an end.

Inside, Dr. King stepped to the pulpit microphone.
He said,

> *There is no stopping point short of victory.*
> *We've got some difficult days ahead.*
> *But it really doesn't matter with me now*
> *because I've been to the mountaintop.*
> *I've seen the Promised Land.*
>
> *I may not get there with you.*
> *But I want you to know tonight*
> *that we, as a people, will get to the Promised Land!*

My daddy rushed home,
charged with emotion,
stumbling over his words,
talking about how good the speech was
and that Dr. King had asked people
to leave their jobs and schools to march.

Daddy was ready to march again.
Me too.

APRIL 4, 1968

No need for a second snooze this morning.
I was too excited, thinking about shopping
after school with my big sister Ruth.
Senior prom was coming up in a couple of weeks
and I wanted to look BEAUTIFUL
for my boyfriend.
We would be the best-looking couple at the prom,
just like last year,
and tomorrow, we would MARCH.

On the number 17 Glenview bus,
I began to map out my day.
First, band practice at seven thirty a.m.
Next, homeroom,
then off to this class and that class
until the day was done.
In my sister's car
we headed for the Southland Mall.
All giggly, filled with energy.

I talked on and on,
not giving Ruth a chance to chime in,
not a word.

Ruth walked and I ran into Goldsmith's,
headed straight for the jewelry department,
went from one counter
to another, looking for the right pair of earrings and
a necklace or two.
Suddenly, an announcement over the radio—

BREAKING NEWS

Around sunset,
Dr. King was gunned down
at the Lorraine Motel
in Memphis, Tennessee.

My own hometown.

AROUND THE WORLD

People were devastated, shocked,
and perplexed.
Ruth and I,
shaken in disbelief,
rushed home,
shouted at the same time,
"Mama, did you hear,
Dr. King has been shot!"

Mama, cookin' and talkin' to herself,
mumbled, "This city is cursed.
They killed a good man.
Why,
why,
why?"

Daddy, his face
crumpled up with grief and anger,
saying over and over,
"If it what'n for bad luck

a Black man wouldn't have no luck
at all."

The telephone rang,
and rang,
and rang.

All across the United States,
mourning
turned into
violence, looting,
burning of property.
I went to the attic
and peered out the window.
It seemed like the sky was on fire.

In the distance,
horns honking,
sirens shrill and wailing.
Fire trucks racing,
ambulances racing,
police cars racing
to stop the mayhem
all night long.

I thought, *Maybe it is true*
what Dr. King said,
"A riot is the language of the unheard."

America, do you hear us now?

APRIL 8, 1968

Sad but strong, Mrs. King,
who had always marched side by side
with her husband,
was determined to carry on his work.

Four days later,
she and three of her young children
led forty-two thousand
spiritually wounded,
grief-stricken,
angry foot soldiers
—including my daddy and me—
through the streets of Memphis.

We marched—
heeding the words of Rev. James Lawson,
a follower of Gandhi's teachings
and a friend of Dr. King,
often called "the mind of the movement."
"March with your head high—with pride:

March SILENTLY in honor of the memory
of Dr. King. Sometimes silence speaks louder
than words."

No chants, no songs,
—for Dr. King,
—for the striking sanitation workers.

Then Mrs. King returned to Atlanta
for her husband's funeral.

Eight days later,
the Negro sanitation strike was over.
The workers had won
higher wages and union recognition.

But sadness loomed
around the world.
Our hearts were heavy.

WHO WOULD LEAD US NOW?

We needed to honor Dr. King
for his sacrifice fighting bigotry, injustice, and hatred.
It was something many people wanted.
But how?

Massachusetts senator Edward Brooke had an idea.
He wrote a bill for a day of commemoration,
remembrance,
like Valentine's Day, St. Patrick's Day, and
Mother's Day.

Unlike **paid** federal holidays,
like George Washington's Birthday,
Memorial Day, and Veterans Day.

Michigan congressman John Conyers
had a better idea.

A few days after Dr. King was assassinated,
he introduced the first bill
for a Martin Luther King Jr. federal holiday.

His bill proposed that every year
on Dr. King's birthday, January 15,
the government and all businesses would close
for a day of celebration,
reflection,
commemoration,
and service.

There was one big problem.

To become a law
the bill would have to pass
through *two* congressional committees:
    the Subcommittee on Census and Population and
    the Committee on Post Office and Civil Service.

Then to the House of Representatives,
    where it needed two hundred and fifty-seven votes.

Then to the Senate,
    where it needed fifty-one votes.

Then to the president's desk
for his signature.
This hurdle seemed insurmountable.
We needed yes votes from both sides,
Republican and Democrat.

MILLIONS OF AMERICANS WANTED A KING HOLIDAY

. . . .

But millions did not.

They said, "He was not a truly great leader."
They said, "It will be too expensive."
They said, "He was Black."
The congressional committees said no!

Representative Conyers and
Representative Shirley Chisholm
were ready to battle hard for the King holiday.
But they realized
it was gonna take a *long* time
to turn the bill into a law.

Yes, it was gonna take a long, long time.

IN THE MEANTIME

The Poor People's Campaign continued.

Foot soldiers across the country would march

to Washington, DC,

with rallies in cities along the way

to protest against hunger and poverty in America,

to demand a twelve-billion-dollar economic bill of rights

Even though Martin Luther King Jr. died, the Poor People's Campaign, which he had spearheaded, continued. These flyers inviting activists to join were distributed at rallies, churches, barbershops, and other community organizations.

for better jobs,
    better homes,
    better education,
    a better life for poor people.

I wanted to help,
make a difference,
change the world,
and honor Dr. King.

I joined the Freedom Choir in Memphis
with some of my friends
and other teens from different schools.

Before the leaders spoke at the local rallies,
we sang
"Oh, Freedom,"
"This Little Light of Mine,"
"Lift Every Voice and Sing,"
and "Ain't Gonna Let Nobody Turn Me 'Round"
to inspire
and encourage.

One speaker said, "We need y'all to march with us to DC."
I knew I had to go.

But Mama and Daddy said, "No.
You are too young to go so far alone."

"But Mama, my friends and classmates are going,
Martha, Cheryl, and Margie."

"It is still too far," Mama said.

"Is it as far as the train ride to Aunt Beatrice's house in
New York City?"

"No; it's about seven hundred miles or so."

"So what, Mama?"

"No, Kathy. Not by yourself."

"You don't understand. I have got to fight for
my people."

Mama looked at me and shook her head.

I was frustrated, inconsolable.
I continued to beg and plead.
I HAD TO GO.

One last try:
I wrote a letter to Mama,

Dear Mom,

I love you very dearly but I wish you would consider the March on Washington. I was so determine to go when I ask daddy, I told him I would run away. But I beg to you to come to the mass meeting Wednesday night & I am sure you would change your mind. I know I said I wouldn't bother you about this. But my heart & soul is set on going to Wash. to help build a shanty town & help solve the economic problem. I guess if I don't go I'll never feel right, it will always be on my conscience. Would you stop for a little while to think about all the poor people the economic problem and we (black) will never see a better day if the parents don't allow the younger generation to help & make their contribution as black people.

please, please, please,

Kathy

This is the actual letter Kathlyn wrote to her mother, begging her to let her go on the Poor People's Campaign bus trip to Washington, DC.

poured my heart and soul onto paper
about my need to work
for CHANGE.

Mama and Daddy read the letter.
I heard them mumbling,
not sure what they would say.
Yes! No! Maybe!
I waited and waited.
Seemed like forever.

At last, they said,
"Yes."

But I had to wear pants.
Boy pants.
Girls didn't wear pants back then.
The only acceptable attire was
skirts, dresses,
and maybe culottes.

And I had to have some money in my pocket.
Daddy often said,
"You should always have a few coins in your pocket
for emergencies."

MAY 2, 1968

Instead of becoming a debutante,
like some of my friends
and other girls my age, or
going to New York City on the senior trip,
like many of my classmates,

Kathlyn was the editor of her high school yearbook. In this photo, she and some of her classmates—from left to right, Patricia Jackson, Lee Etta Rogers, Valeria Alexander, Kathlyn Wiggins, Regina Dodson, Marjorie Bradfield, Joyce Parker, the club adviser, Mrs. T. J. Cooper and Cassandra Hunt—pose in front of buses they would take for an educational school trip to New York City at the end of the year. However, because Kathlyn and Marjorie became foot soldiers and went on the Poor People's Campaign to Washington, DC, they didn't end up going on the the senior girls trip.

I got on a double-decker bus
called the Freedom Train—
the first caravan of
the Poor People's Campaign.

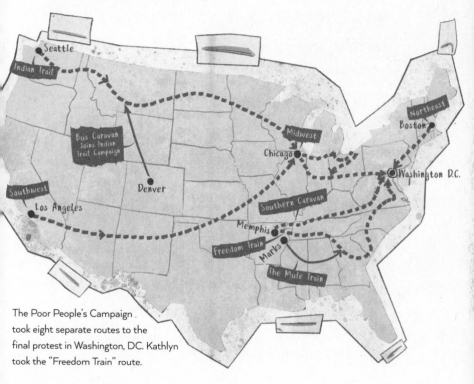

The Poor People's Campaign
took eight separate routes to the
final protest in Washington, DC. Kathlyn
took the "Freedom Train" route.

Foot soldiers came from all over
on different caravans.
There were eight all together.
We traveled from city to city,
marching and holding rallies.

The Freedom Train took us to
some places that I had never been before—
    Marx, Mississippi;
    Nashville and Knoxville, Tennessee;
    Raleigh, North Carolina;
    Danville, Virginia—
and right into Washington, DC,
marching and singing Negro spirituals,
including my favorite:
Ain't gonna let nobody turn me 'round,
    turn me 'round,
    turn me 'round.
Ain't gonna let nobody
    turn me 'round.

Keep on a-walkin',
    keep on a-talkin',
Marchin' on to freedom land.

IT DIDN'T MATTER

· ·

Congress did nothing.

No economic justice for the poor.
No economic bill of rights
for those seeking and needing to work,
for those disabled and unable to work,
for those needing fair and decent housing.

Tired and frustrated by the lack of progress
and disorganization,
my friends Cheryl and Margie and I
marched and rallied all the way to DC.
Then we left the Poor People's Campaign.

I returned home, graduated from high school,
and headed for Memphis State University.

AUGUST 1968

. . . .

I arrived at college and
EVERY DAY
when we stepped off
the number 5 central bus,
heading for class,
the first thing me and my friends saw,
hanging from the Kappa Alpha fraternity house,
was a big old Confederate flag.
A symbol for
    hate,
    slavery,
    racism, and
    White supremacy.

Still a foot soldier, I joined the Black
Students' Association.

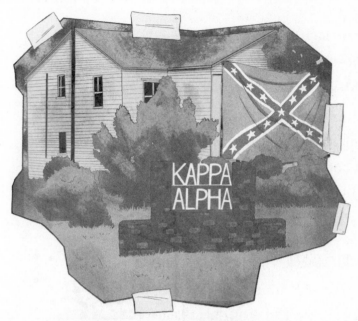

Kappa Alpha had a two-story Confederate flag hanging from its fraternity house on the Memphis State University campus in 1968.

We protested again and again and again.

"Why no Black-history classes?"

"Why only one Negro professor?"

"Why is there a Confederate flag two stories high hanging from a campus fraternity house's portico?"

That same year, in spite of Congress,
Mrs. King and the Martin Luther King Jr. Center for Nonviolent Social Change

in Atlanta, Georgia,
started to recognize and observe Dr. King's birthday
with an ecumenical service that brought different
religions together,
educational programs, policy seminars,
and other events,
calling for a national observance of
Dr. King's birthday.

A few years later, in spite of Congress,
the city of Washington, DC, moved ahead
to make Dr. King's birthday, January 15,
a legal holiday.
The state of Illinois was next.
Massachusetts and Connecticut followed.

1971

· ·

Three years after the first bill was proposed,
the Congressional Black Caucus
sent out a call for action to foot soldiers from
all walks of life—
social and civic organizations,
fraternities,
sororities,
unions,
and churches—
to pressure Congress to say **YES**
to the Dr. Martin Luther King Jr. holiday bill.

And the Southern Christian Leadership
Conference initiated
the first **nationwide petition**
for a Martin Luther King Jr. federal holiday.

Foot soldiers wrote resolutions,
marched in parades,

wore special T-shirts, and
sent letters to Congress.

Three million signatures were collected
in support of a King holiday.

Still, Congress lagged, stalled, questioned, and debated.
Talk, talk, talk;
No, no, no.

The foot soldiers fought on.

NOT ME

· ·

Not yet.
I found a good job in Buffalo, New York,
volunteered at a hospital,
went back to school,
found love,
got married.

While I was living my life,
Congress convened again and again.
The legislators agreed, disagreed, repeated, and appealed.
Still, nothing moved the bill out of committee.
Not a plea from the National Council of Churches.
Not Mrs. King's testimony before the
Senate Judiciary Committee.
Not requests from joint hearings of Congress.
Not three hundred thousand more petition signatures.

Nothing would sway them.

1979

· ·

More talk, talk, talk.

One opponent said,
"Dr. King made anti-American statements,"
because he spoke out against the Vietnam War.
Another said,
"Only two men, Christopher Columbus
and George Washington,
have been honored with a federal holiday . . .
the discoverer of America
and the Founding Father of our country."
He said Dr. King did not measure up to these
two great men.
Others said,
"A commemorative day for Dr. King is . . .
not [an] appropriate way to honor him."
"The cost to enact another legal holiday—
ASTRONOMICAL!"

But like an active volcano,
pressure mounted for the King holiday.
More foot soldiers joined the movement.
(But not me!
Not yet!)

Finally, in a written supplement to his
State of the Union address,
President Jimmy Carter spoke up.
"Dr. Martin Luther King, Jr. led this Nation's effort to
provide all its citizens with civil rights
and equal opportunities . . . It is appropriate that
his birthday be commemorated as a national holiday . . .
I will support legislation."

His support brought momentum.

AFTER TEN YEARS

The King holiday bill passed
through the committees to the House floor.
Finally.

Made a lot of folks glad.
But not enough.

On the House floor,
talk, talk, talk.
King was a good man.
Talk, talk, talk.
King was a bad man.

Time to vote.
Two hundred and fifty-two yeas.
One hundred and thirty-three nays.

Five votes short.
Just five.

Made us SO mad.
But not for long.

Frustrated, Mrs. King
and the Congressional Black Caucus knew they needed
a different kind of warrior.
Someone who could inspire, awaken, electrify.

Aha!

Stevie Wonder—
singer, songwriter, musician, social activist.
He had worked for years with Mrs. King, and then . . .

SEPTEMBER 1980

Stevie released an album,

Hotter Than July,

with a song pleading for the King federal holiday.

Why has there never been a holiday, yeah,

Where peace is celebrated . . .

Stevie Wonder's album *Hotter Than July*, which has the
"Happy Birthday" song in honor of Martin Luther King Jr.

I bought the album,
played it over and over.
Oh, I loved "Happy Birthday,"
which some call the "Black Happy Birthday song."
It thrilled me, moved me, inspired me.

Still no King holiday,
but no matter.

Every year
on January 15,
foot soldiers across the world
sang Stevie's "Happy Birthday."

On that day, we celebrated,
attended programs and services,
and engaged in community service activities
anyway.

OCTOBER 31, 1980

· ·

The Hotter Than July concert tour kicked off
in Houston, Texas.
Stevie sang Dr. King's holiday anthem
    live
for the first time.

The crowd shouted and sang,
"Happy birthday to you
Happy birthday to you . . .
Happy birthday."

Between tour dates, supported by the
Congressional Black Caucus,
Stevie spearheaded, funded, and planned
the Dr. Martin Luther King holiday march,
a huge rally and benefit concert
in Washington, DC.

Tireless, Stevie opened an office
and hired lobbyists who would
pressure Congress to vote
   YES
for the King holiday bill.

The King Center joined in the effort.
More shows, more cities followed.
Thousands were inspired.
They joined the movement
and became foot soldiers.

MY LIFE WAS FULL

Married, one child,
working and going to school.

Still, something was missing.

I longed to be back in the movement.
I yearned to be fighting for a BIG cause.
This time, I wanted
to recruit,
to march,
to help make
Dr. Martin Luther King Jr.'s holiday
a reality.

I thought again and again about
my first march, the 1968 sanitation workers' strike,
my first nationwide protest, the Poor People's Campaign,
and my college days, when I protested for Black faculty
and against the racism on campus and in the classroom.

I was ready to be a foot soldier again.

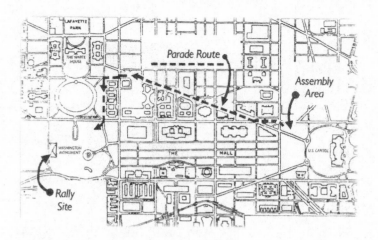

STEVIE WONDER'S MARCH
ON WASHINGTON D.C.
JANUARY 15th
FOR DR. MARTIN LUTHER KING JR. DAY
TO BECOME A NATIONAL HOLIDAY.

11:00 AM   ASSEMBLY AT U.S. CAPITOL BUILDING.
1:00 PM   RALLY ON THE WEST SLOPE OF THE
WASHINGTON MONUMENT.

JOIN STEVIE WONDER IN WASHINGTON D.C. ON JANUARY 15th.
HELP HIS DREAM BECOME A REALITY.

SEE OTHER SIDE FOR PARADE ROUTE MAP.

The flyer for
Stevie Wonder's
march, January
15, 1981.

JANUARY 15, 1981

In freezing cold, sleet, and snow,
one hundred thousand foot soldiers—including my mama,
my sister Carolyn, and ME—
marched from the U.S. Capitol Building to the
Washington Monument
chanting: "We want a holiday . . .
a Martin Luther King Day!"

Kathlyn, her mom, Mrs. Wiggins, and her sister Carolyn,
and Kathlyn with other foot soldiers in Washington, DC.

It felt so good standing shoulder to shoulder
with fellow foot soldiers,
marching, singing, protesting.

Foot soldiers from all over the United States convened in
Washington, DC, demanding the King holiday.

From a far distance we could see the stage with
about thirty or forty famous and not-so-famous people:
Stevie's mama, Mrs. Lula Hardaway;
Martin Luther King III;
soul and jazz poet and musician Gil Scott-Heron;

Stevie Wonder speaking to the foot soldiers at the King Holiday Rally in Washington, DC, January 15, 1981, from left to right: Gil Scott Heron, Stevie Wonder, Rev. Jesse Jackson, Gladys Knight, and Rep. John Conyers.

singers Gladys Knight and Johnny Taylor;

DC mayor Marion Barry;

Representatives John Conyers and Walter Fauntroy;

activists Dick Gregory and Jesse Jackson;

and a lot more.

We listened as Stevie spoke.

"Designating his birthday a national holiday would create an event for all Americans . . . So when you return to your cities, your homes, your jobs, please carry on the vigil." Spread across the snow-covered field, we sang "Happy Birthday."

Then we headed home—north, south, east, and west.
Boots on the ground for the King holiday.

NEVER LET THE DREAM DIE
...CONTINUE THE STRUGGLE.

February 15, 1981

*One month ago today
we joined as one to remind America
that we have not forgotten
Dr. Martin Luther King, Jr.'s Dream.*

*My heartfelt thanks for your
concern, participation and support
to help make his birthday
an official National Holiday.*

Stevie Wonder

A thank-you card Kathlyn received as a coordinator
for the Stevie Wonder March on Washington rally:
Never let the dream die . . . Continue the struggle.

NINE DAYS LATER

· ·

Stevie Wonder would be in Buffalo.
My childhood heartthrob!
The teenage girl's crush was gone
(well, mostly),
replaced with deep admiration
and respect.

I had to meet him to tell him so.
But I didn't know how.

Pondering and pacing by day,
tossing and turning all night.
Then, like a flash of lightning, the answer came:

Call Lil Mary,
my former homeroom teacher, church member, and
adviser to our high-school girls' club, the Gems.
That's what we affectionately called Mrs. Mary Nichols,
because she was so cool.
She would know exactly what to do, especially

since she had become the co-owner of Top Tickets,
an entertainment and promotion ticket-sales venue.
The first African American woman to do so.

"Lil Mary, Stevie is coming to town and I got to
meet him.

What do I do?"

DECKED OUT IN FUR COAT AND PEARLS

With Anaxet, my two-year-old, on my hip,
drowning in jitters,
I took a deep breath and
introduced myself to Stevie as a minister's wife.
MESMERIZED!
I took lots of pictures with my Kodak Instamatic.

Headed home,
with Anaxet strapped in the car seat,
still floating on cloud nine.
In a dreamy state of distraction,
I drove off.

But my camera was on top of the car.

BAM!

It smashed to smithereens,
picture memories in the wind.

THE SILVER LINING

· ·

With two complimentary tickets in hand,
I braved the cold again,
this time with my friend Cheryl,
for the Hotter Than July concert
at Buffalo Memorial Auditorium.

And at the concert,
we sang *so* loud and me a bit off-key:
"Happy birthday to you,
Happy birthday to you,

Hap-py birrthdaay."

Then I took a picture with Stevie.

HUZZAH!

Kathlyn poses with Stevie Wonder after
his concert in Buffalo, New York, in 1981.

STEVIE TOURED ON

And foot soldiers worked hard.
Petitions went out across the country,
to civil rights groups,
local and national labor unions,
churches,
sororities and fraternities.

Loaded down with a stack of petitions,
I gave a pile to friends
and a bunch to my family.

We foot soldiers went everywhere,
spoke to anybody,
at barbershops,
at beauty shops,
even at bus stops.
"Sign here, please!"

Tired, weary, and worn,
but determined,
Mama, Carolyn, and I collected thousands of signatures.

A Petition to the United States Congress

We, the undersigned believe that, in the interest of improved human relations in our country, there should be a national holiday honoring a black American. We believe further, that Dr. Martin Luther King, Jr. dedicated his life to justice, equality and brotherhood for all Americans, Black and white and that Dr. King's life and work represent the highest patriotism and the very spirit of democracy.

We therefore hereby petition the United States Congress to enact legislation providing for the establishment of January 15, the birthday of Dr. Martin Luther King, Jr., as a national holiday.

NAME	ADDRESS	ZIP

Tear out, fill out (photocopy if more space is needed) and mail to:
The Martin Luther King, Jr. Center for Social Change
503 Auburn Ave., N.E.
Atlanta, Georgia 30312

A copy of the original petition to the U.S. Congress, requesting it enact a national holiday in honor of Martin Luther King Jr., spearheaded by the Martin Luther King Jr. Center for Nonviolent Social Change.

FEBRUARY 23, 1982

Mrs. King and Stevie
appeared at a congressional committee hearing.
They delivered *seven million signatures,*
the most *ever* in support of a bill.

Still, opponents criticized and attacked.

"Honoring King is especially a disgrace, dishonor, and
betrayal of the 56,234 men who died in Vietnam."
"Reverend King was collaborating with and being
manipulated by Communists."
"Cost the taxpayers five hundred million dollars or
more a year."

More talk, talk, talk.
More no, no, no.
Made us sad!
Made us mad!

No matter.
Ain't gonna let nobody turn US 'round.

1983

. . . .

A new Congress with new members.

Representative Conyers introduced
ANOTHER bill, H.R. 800.
This bill had a lot more cosponsors,
eighty-eight in all,
Democrats and Republicans,
the most ever.

At last, the wheels of change began to turn.
Many in Congress
began to soften
to the idea of a King holiday.

The House Subcommittee on Census and Population
convened—AGAIN.

But one problem just wouldn't go away.

To honor Dr. King on his actual birthday
would create an annual floating holiday.

Government offices and buildings
would have to open and close
twice in one week.
The cost for overtime
and lost work time would be **enormous,**
about eighteen million dollars some estimated.

But WAIT!
Indiana Democrat and
foot soldier Representative Katie Hall
brought a new idea—a COMPROMISE.
Instead of the fixed date of January 15,
she wrote a bill, H.R. 3345,
    "to designate the <u>third Monday in January each year</u> a
legal public holiday to commemorate the birthday of
Dr. Martin Luther King, Jr."

Her bill
would create a fixed three-day weekend instead of a
floating holiday.
Her bill
would halt the dual opening and closing of government offices.
Her bill
would save the government money,

98TH CONGRESS
1ST SESSION
H. R. 3345

To amend title 5, United States Code, to make the birthday of Martin Luther King, Junior, a legal public holiday.

IN THE HOUSE OF REPRESENTATIVES

JUNE 16, 1983

Mrs. HALL of Indiana (for herself, Mr. UDALL, Mr. FORD of Michigan, Mr. CLAY, Mrs. SCHROEDER, Mr. GARCIA, Mr. LELAND, Ms. OAKAR, Mr. DELLUMS, Mr. MITCHELL, Mr. RANGEL, Mrs. COLLINS, Mr. DIXON, Mr. GRAY, Mr. OWENS, and Mr. TOWNS) introduced the following bill; which was referred to the Committee on Post Office and Civil Service

---

A BILL

To amend title 5, United States Code, to make the birthday of Martin Luther King, Junior, a legal public holiday.

1   *Be it enacted by the Senate and House of Representa-*

2   *tives of the United States of America in Congress assembled,*

3   That section 6103(a) of title 5, United States Code, is

4   amended by inserting immediately below the item relating to

5   New Year's Day the following:

6   "Birthday of Martin Luther King, Junior, the

7   third Monday in January.".

8   SEC. 2. The amendment made by the first section of this

The first page of the compromise bill calling for a Martin Luther King Jr. holiday, initiated by Representative Katie Hall, with an amendment changing the date of the holiday from his actual birthday of January 15 to the third Monday in January.

LOTS of money—millions.

Suddenly, other House members wanted to be cosponsors.
Representative Katie Hall worked
faster and
harder.
She introduced a second bill
and added a hundred and eight more signatures.

At last, the bill got out of committee and headed to
the full House.
Although she was a junior Congress member,
Representative Hall was selected to serve as
the floor manager
and she took a bold step:
"Mr. Speaker, I move to suspend the rules and pass the bill
H.R. 3706 to amend title 5 . . . to make the birthday of
Martin Luther King, Jr. a legal holiday."
The debate was lively, energetic.
Three hundred and thirty-eight yeas, ninety nays.
The yeas have it!

NEXT UP: THE SENATE

· ·

Before the vote,
many foot soldiers,
Mrs. King,
and her son Martin Luther King III,
anxious yet hopeful,
gathered at the Capitol for a
prayer vigil.

The bill went to the Senate floor.
The momentum good,
until North Carolina Republican senator Jesse Helms
staged a filibuster
for sixteen days.

He gave long speeches
to delay, distract, and stonewall
the vote for the Dr. Martin Luther King holiday.
He even passed out a three-hundred-page FBI report
about Dr. King,

calling him a Communist and many other bad things.

"Inaccurate and false," said one senator.

"Filth," said another as he threw his copy to the floor.

The filibuster didn't work.

OCTOBER 19, 1983

SHE GOT KING HIS DAY!

Indiana Representative Katie Hall came up with the idea for celebrating Martin Luther King's birthday on the third Monday in January.

The bill was "considered and passed," seventy-eight to twenty-two.

HALLELUJAH!

Two weeks later,
Mrs. King, Representative Katie Hall,
and many foot soldiers
witnessed President Reagan sign
the King Bill into public law.

I saw it on the evening news.
I read it in
the *Buffalo News* and

President Reagan signs the bill to enact a Martin Luther King Jr. national holiday into law, November 2, 1983. Standing with him in the Rose Garden ceremony from left to right are Vice President George H. W. Bush; Mrs. Coretta Scott King; Representative Katie Hall (D-Ind.); Samuel Pierce, secretary of housing and urban development; J. Steven Rhodes, the vice president's domestic policy assistant; and Senator Howard Baker of Tennessee.

the *Challenger,* our own Black newspaper.
It was hard to believe.

I called my mama and sister Carolyn,
chanting and singing,
off-key again.
"We got a holiday,
a Martin Luther King Day.
Happy birthday to you,
happy birthday to you,

hap-py birrthdaay . . ."

We remembered
the march led by Stevie Wonder,
how much fun we had,
we laughed and even cried
tears of joy.

Although it would take another three years
for Martin Luther King Day to be an
official federal holiday,
a compromise by the House
and the Senate,
we were thankful.

JANUARY 1986

Many had waited for this moment
to celebrate.

I took my daughters to Shea's Buffalo Theatre,
to see *Living the Dream,*
a tribute to Dr. King,
sponsored by Buffalo's Martin Luther King
Celebration committee.

Tradition was born that night.
For many years to come,
my family braved the wind, cold, and
sometimes heavy snow
to celebrate Dr. King's birthday
with friends, family, and others who cherished
Dr. King's memory—
together.

THROUGH YEARS OF TALK, TALK, TALK

And NO, NO, NO,
we persevered!

We made Dr. Martin Luther King Jr.'s holiday a reality.
Honoring the man
Who preached nonviolence—in the face of violence.
Who marched in peace—in the face of rage.
Who fought for freedom—in the face of captivity.

He did it for love—and so did we.
He did it for justice—and so did we.
He did it for equality—and so did we.

You don't know our faces.
You don't know our names.
But for FIFTEEN YEARS
we foot soldiers

—just ordinary, everyday people—
carried on all across the U.S.A.
ever ready
to press on,
march on,
stand firm, and sacrifice
until victory was won—

not lettin' nobody turn us 'round.

01

Kathlyn at age ten in her Easter frock with her brothers Michael (age five) and Mack Carlos (age eleven).

03

The Poor People's Campaign Freedom Choir in Marx, Mississippi.

02

04

Kathlyn with her Gem sisters at their club adviser Lil Mary's house. Lil Mary was Kathlyn's English teacher and the senior class adviser. She called Kathlyn and her friends "her gems," and eventually the group of girls became a club that has continued to this day. From left to right, poised on the floor: Martha Porter, Glenda Robinson, Cassandra Hunt, Jenise Cumby. Sitting from left to right: Rita Young, Joyce Parker, Phyllis London, Wanda Taylor, Marjorie Bradfield, adviser, Mary Nichols. Standing: Danette Jones, Kathlyn Wiggins, Charlotte Walker. Cropped into the photo, from top to bottom, are headshots of Gem sisters Linda Brown, Janice Jones, and Cheryl Fanion.

Kathlyn with her boyfriend, Alan, now her husband, dressed up for her junior prom. (Her senior prom was canceled due to the mayhem after Dr. King's death.)

06

07

Kathlyn, still in college, visiting her
sister in New York with a bigger,
bolder Afro. ◄········

Kathlyn's first Afro, when she
was in college.

05

08

Kathlyn while in grad school at
the University of Wisconsin–
Madison. ◄·········

Kathlyn's high school
senior portrait.

09

Soul sister Kathlyn (left) with her brother Mack Carlos (right) and his friend, posing in front of a 1970 Buick Opel GT, pretending to own this "cool" sports car.

12

Stevie Wonder speaking to news media and foot soldiers after the 1981 march.

10

A headshot of Kathlyn when she was selected by New York Telephone to receive an award from the Urban League. Her daughter Anaxet calls it her "pretty lady" photo.

11

Foot soldiers from Howard University School of Law participating in Stevie Wonder's 1981 march for Martin Luther King Jr.'s holiday.

AUTHOR'S NOTE

We have bent and bent and bent . . . we are through bending.

—MACK C. WIGGINS

The seeds of this book lay dormant for decades and began to grow only when I became an oral storyteller, sharing my days of civil rights activism as a youth and as an adult in a workshop called How Dr. King's Day Came to Be. On one occasion, as I was wrapping up a workshop, Jeanne Arradondo, a friend and former fellow church member, said, "You should write a book." That statement echoed in my subconscious for years. Although the seed was planted a decade or so ago, I had other writing projects rambling in my head that I thought were more important. In 2015, after much prodding from my daughter Anaxet, I refocused and turned all of my attention and a great deal of my time to researching and writing this book, which required a vast amount of time and energy, more than I spent completing my doctoral dissertation. Seven years later, I'm finally ready to share my story with the world.

When I decided to focus on this book, I had no idea that my family and the adventures in my own life would inspire me so much, primarily because I was living in a bubble I call Kathy's World.

In Kathy's World, like many kids, I had a fantastic childhood. I didn't even realize that we were poor until I was about twenty-eight years old. Kathy's World was a place of merriment and self-made fantasy. I loved everything about my bubble, like rolling down the steps at White Stone Baptist Church with my friend Linda during kindergarten recess and going to the New Daisy Theatre on Beale Street with my family. That's the famous street where I participated in my very first protest march, where the blues was born, where the Cotton Makers Jubilee carnival was held. I was shielded from the separate and very unequal ideology of segregation and Jim Crow. Thank you, Mama and Daddy.

However, Kathy's World shattered into a million pieces on April 4, 1968, the day Dr. King was murdered.

Although I had many twists and turns before becoming a foot soldier, it was really just a matter of time. I now realize that activism is in my DNA. My parents and siblings, each with a different type of dedication and commitment in their efforts to change the world, helped me grow and spread my wings.

My daddy marched and spoke out, not only for the sanitation strikers, but for himself and other Black business owners as they fought against the government takeover disguised as Urban Renewal on Beale Street. Although they were unsuccessful in their bid to save Beale Street from gentrification, they fought until the end. Sadly, many of the historical sites on Beale Street, including my daddy's business, Wiggins and Sons' Barbershop, are now only distant memories and images shelved in the Memphis Public Library photo archives.

My mother's passion, however, was for voter registration. During my childhood, Mama was a poll worker at every election, many times after finishing an eight- or twelve-hour shift as a private-duty nurse. Mama was adamant that we all must vote. It was our moral and civic duty. I called her to check in one day before leaving Memphis State to hang out with my friends and she told me not to come home until I had registered to vote and that I should take my friends with me. I did, and I have voted in every election for the past five decades.

My big sister Ruth, a student herself, worked in the cafeteria at Tennessee State University. She, like most of the students there, was the first generation of her family to attend college. Money for most was tight. I am sure this was against school policy, but Ruth allowed many of her hungry classmates to eat even when they had no money to pay for their meals. Decades later, I went with her to a TSU homecoming, and the first words from some of her former classmates' mouths were "Thank you, Ruth. We never would have made it without you."

And big sister Carolyn was one of the publicly faceless and nameless TSU students arrested for participating at the sit-in at the Woolworth counter in Nashville, Tennessee, under the leadership of Marion Barry, who would go on to become the mayor of Washington, DC. I was nine years old and vividly recall watching the Sunday evening news and seeing my sister and other TSU students being loaded into a police paddy wagon.

After watching my parents and sisters stand firm on the battlefield for various causes, I learned that you don't have to be famous to make a difference. Ordinary, everyday people with committed spirits and determined hearts can change the world.

I am still on the battlefield, lesser known to most but still a doer, a worker, one of many foot soldiers, this time working with my husband to eradicate illiteracy. We bring books to life for minority and disadvantaged youth. When I look into their eyes, I see creativity and imagination being stifled in a hopelessness that we are determined to reverse. We ain't gonna let nobody turn us 'round.

My hope is that in reading this book, you realize that anybody can be an activist, an advocate, and a champion with passion for a cause. Yes, even you. May you be so moved and inspired to create or find a cause, a movement that will light your fire to work, to fight—for positive change in this great world we live in.

GLOSSARY

Bill: A draft of a proposed law that is presented to Congress for discussion and debate and voted on by the legislature—the Senate or the House of Representatives. If passed, the bill must then be approved by the executive, the president.

Bill Clerk: Receives, organizes, and processes all official documents, e.g., introduced bills and resolutions, amendments, and names of additional cosponsors.

Congress: Every two years, citizens of the United States elect individuals to represent them in the House of Representatives; every six years, they elect new senators. The House and the Senate make up the national legislative body, which meets at the Capitol Building in Washington, DC, to introduce bills and make laws for citizens.

Democrat: One of the two major political parties in the United States. The party color is blue and the donkey is the party symbol. Democrats support increased government oversight and assistance for citizens. They are typically more liberal on social issues.

Draft: An early, initial, or basic sketch of a written document such as a bill—e.g., H.R. 16510, the first bill written for a Dr. Martin Luther King Jr. holiday.

Enrolling Clerks: These clerks draft messages to the Senate regarding any passed legislation, such as laws, statutes, and acts; they also prepare the official engrossed copies of all House-passed measures, like the Dr. Martin Luther King Bill, and the official enrollment of all House-designated measures that have passed both the Senate and the House of Representatives.

House of Representatives: Makes and passes federal laws as established in the Constitution. The House is the lower legislative house of the U.S. Congress. (The upper house is the U.S. Senate.) There can be no more than four hundred and thirty-five voting members proportionally representing the citizens of the fifty states. To be elected to the House, you must be at least twenty-five years old, have been a U.S. citizen for at least seven years, and be a resident of the state from which you were elected.

Journal Clerks: These clerks collect and organize the daily minutes of the House proceedings and publish them in the *House Journal* at the conclusion of each session. The *House Journal* is the official record of the proceedings as established by the Constitution.

Law: Rules voted on and created by Congress. An example is Public Law 98-144, Ninety-Eighth Congress, an Act to make the birthday of Martin Luther King Jr. a legal public holiday.

Reading Clerks: These clerks read all bills, resolutions, amendments, motions, and messages from the president that come to the House; they also report to the Senate all legislative actions taken by the House.

Republican: One of the two major political parties in the United States. The party color is red and the elephant is the party symbol. The Republican Party is also known as the Grand Old Party (GOP). They advocate for reduced government spending and oversight and greater private and individual control. They are typically more conservative on social issues.

Senate: Responsible for all lawmaking in the United States with the House. In order for a bill or act to be valid, both legislative branches must approve the identical document. The Senate has the important role of ratifying treaties with a two-thirds majority of all senators present and a majority rule for public appointments (e.g., cabinet members, ambassadors, and justices of the Supreme Court). The Senate also adjudicates the official decision as it relates to impeachment proceedings initiated by the House of Representatives with a two-thirds majority vote.

Speaker of the House: The party leader, Democrat or Republican, presides over debates and appoints members to committees. The Speaker is the second in line, after the vice president, to become president.

Tally Clerks: These clerks operate the electronic voting system, record votes taken on the House floor, receive reports of committees, and prepare the calendar of the House of Representatives.

HOW A BILL BECOMES A LAW

A new law can be inspired by anyone. Yes, even you!
Imagine you want your birthday to be declared a federal holiday.
Here is how you do it!

1 **You Have an Idea for a New Law!**

2 You **Draft a Bill,** which means you write a description of your idea for Congress.

3 Next, **Get a Sponsor,** a member of Congress, to introduce the bill.

4 The sponsor will **Find Cosponsors,** other members of Congress who support it.

5 The sponsor and cosponsors will **Introduce the Bill to the House of Representatives,** telling all the representatives about it.

6 First, they **Put the Bill in the Hopper,** a special box next to the desk of the bill clerk (a person who takes care of the official papers of Congress).

7 Then, the bill clerk will **Assign a Number** to the bill to keep track of it.

8 Finally, the reading clerk (a person who reads all official papers to the House of Representatives) will **Read the Bill** to the House.

9 The Speaker of the House, who leads the House, will **Assign the Bill to a Committee,** a group of representatives who are experts on a specific topic. The bill is added to their calendar.

17 The Speaker of the House asks the representatives to **Vote on the Bill.**

18 If two-thirds of the House votes for the bill, it is **Referred to the Senate.**

15 The bill is finalized, **Scheduled for Floor Action,** and added to the legislative calendar. The Speaker of the House decides when and in what order bills will be read.

16 The reading clerk reads the bill to the full House, one section at a time. The representatives **Debate the Bill** and recommend any changes.

14 The committee chair's staff **Publishes a Report** about the bill: what it does, how much it will cost, and how it is supported and/or opposed by committee members.

13 The committee discusses and votes on the revised bill. If they vote yes, **The Bill Is "Ordered Reported,"** and they prepare to move it back to the House for a vote.

12 The subcommittee will **"Mark Up" the Bill,** making changes. If they still think the bill is a good idea, they provide a report to the full committee. If not, the bill "dies."

10 If the committee needs more information, they **Form a Subcommittee.** (If the subcommittee does not take any action, the bill does not move forward and it "dies.")

11 The subcommittee researches the bill and often holds **Hearings,** meetings where experts, supporters, and opponents publicly comment about why the bill is a good or bad idea.

19 The vice president, referred to as the presiding officer, leads the Senate and **Assigns the Bill to a Committee,** a group of senators who are experts on the topic. The bill repeats the same process as in the House (see steps 10–16).

20 Sometimes, a senator will try to **Filibuster,** which means they try to block a Senate vote by talking about the bill for a very long time or using other delay tactics.

21 The vice president initiates the roll call for the senators to **Vote on the Bill.**

22 If both the House and Senate vote for the bill, they **Create a Conference Report,** with recommendations by the House and Senate that must be accepted by both.

23 Congress will **Send the Bill to the President** of the United States. The president can 1) sign the bill, 2) veto the bill, or 3) do nothing. (If the president does nothing and Congress is not in session, the bill "dies." This is called a **pocket veto.**)

24 If the president vetoes the Bill, Congress can **Override the Veto,** but only if both the House and Senate have a two-thirds majority present at roll call.

25 If 1) the president signs the bill, 2) Congress overrides the president's veto, or 3) the president does nothing for ten days *and* Congress is in session, then **The Bill Becomes a Law** (finally!) and the federal government enforces it. Congratulations!

ACKNOWLEDGMENTS

The many individuals who helped me shape and write my first children's book have blessed me immeasurably. It was not luck or a coincidence that our paths crossed; it was divine design, and for that I give praise and thanksgiving. A mere thank-you seems pale in comparison to all the effort, professional support, research hours, and prayers extended on my behalf as I worked to convert the innumerable drafts into a polished product.

For my firstborn, **Anaxet Yvette Jones,** my very first editor, tech person, and burden bearer, thank you for pushing me to dig deeper and for insisting that I put my other writing projects aside to finish this book. To my dutiful daughter **Juliette Marie Jones,** I so appreciate your immense encouragement, which even today is beyond measure. And to my soul mate, helpmate, and beloved husband, **Alan P.,** thank you for being my rock and superman.

No words can express my esteem, respect, and indebtedness to my first professional editor, now literary agent and friend, **Janna Morishima,** who saw the potential of this manuscript and saw something in me—yes, even at my age—and was willing to invest years and years of time and energy, offering "real" good advice, as we walked, worked, and journeyed together, determined to make my literary dream a reality. And thank you to **Dimitrea Tokumbo** for linking us together; my heart brims over with gratitude for the both of you.

I am overcome with joy and ever so grateful to my favorite writer, author extraordinaire **Jacqueline Woodson,** for penning the foreword to my book and for her most generous and insightful mentorship. And thanks to musical genius **Toshi Reagon** for bringing our souls together.

Many, many thanks to my splendiferous Versify team, led by **Kwame Alexander,** at Clarion Books, especially editor **Erika Turner,** who felt my heart and affirmed my vision with a *yes,* and **Ciera Burch,** whose nonstop efforts helped me get to and *over* the finish line. To illustrator **Steffi Walthall,** book designer **Natalie Fondriest,** and infographic creator **Chenjelani Whatley,** thank you for lending your genius to breathe life into my story. And endless gratitude to Editorial Director, **Emilia Rhodes,** for being an advocate of my work and story and helping to manifest the vision of this book to fruition.

Special thanks to my Highlights Foundation instructors and authors **Deborah Hopkinson,** who offered constructive critiques and suggested that I pen my story in verse, and **Jan Field** and **Pamela Turner,** who provided great feedback in the early stages as I transitioned from the scholarly writing of academia to children's literature.

Thanks overflow to the people and many institutions that provided archival documents and answers to a host of questions; your research efforts are priceless: **Katherine Mollan,** from the Center for Legislative Archives, National Archives and Records Administration; Benjamin L. Hooks Central Library, History Department; Buffalo and Erie County Public Library; Congressional Research Services; Stuart A. Rose Manuscript, Archives, and Rare Book Library at Emory University; Jimmy Carter Presidential Library and Museum; Prints and Photograph Divisions, Researcher and Reference Services Division at Library of Congress; Tennessee State Library Archives; U. S. House of Representatives Office of the Historian; and the University of Memphis's Preservation and Special Collections Department at the University Libraries.

A big shout-out to my bestie since kindergarten, **Linda Brown Williams,** for unfailingly promoting me and the book from day one while also serving as my personal historian. I thank you and my other Gem sisters **Cheryl Fanion Cotton, Margie Bradfield Morgan, Glenda Robinson Oates,** and **Cassandra Hunt Thompson** for helping me recall some funny and important moments that had become faded memories.

Much love and appreciation to my brother **Michael Wiggins** for giving me room to breathe. And finally to a host of family, friends, and supporters who prayed and provided encouragement along the way. You know who you are; thank you so much. All I can say is, I'm much obliged!

SOURCE NOTES

AIN'T GONNA LET NOBODY TURN ME 'ROUND
Arrangement by Bernice Johnson Reagon
© 2000 Songtalk Publishing Co., Washington, DC
International Copyright Secured Made in U.S.A.
All Rights Reserved Including Public Performance For Profit
Used by Permission

BIBLIOGRAPHY

African American Voices in Congress. "Text of Stevie Wonder's Speech
Advocating a National Martin Luther King Jr. Holiday." African American
Voices in Congress, www.avoiceonline.org/mlk-holiday-edu/assets/speech-
text_stevie-wonder.pdf.

Allen, Carl. "Area Events to Mark National Holiday for King." *Buffalo News,*
January 14, 1986.

———. "At City Hall, King Holiday Is Business as Usual." *Buffalo News,*
January 15, 1986.

Ayres, Alex, ed. *The Wisdom of Martin Luther King Jr.* Meridian, OH:
Palatino, 1993.

Barm, Marcus. "How Stevie Wonder Helped Create Martin Luther King
Day." Medium.com, January 18, 2015, medium.com/cuepoint/how-stevie-
wonder-helped-create-martin-luther-king-day-807451a78664.

Benjamin L. Hooks Institute for Social Change. "1968, the Sanitation Workers and Dr. King." University of Memphis, www.memphis.edu/benhooks/mapping-civil-rights/1968.php.

A Bill to Make the Birthday of Martin Luther King, Junior, a Legal Public Holiday, H.R. 16510, 90th Congress (1968).

A Bill to Designate the Birthday of Martin Luther King, Junior, a Legal Public Holiday, H.R. 800, 98th Congress (1983).

A Bill to Amend Title 5, United States Code, to Make the Birthday of Martin Luther King, Junior, a Legal Public Holiday, H.R. 3706, 98th Congress (1983).

A Bill to Amend Title 5, United States Code, to Make the Birthday of Martin Luther King, Junior, a Legal Public Holiday, H.R. 3345, 98th Congress (1983).

"Birthday Celebration for M.L.K." *Ebony* (March 1981): 127–29.

Bond, Beverly G., and Janann Sherman. *Memphis in Black and White.* Charleston: Arcadia, 2003.

Carter, Jimmy. State of the Union Annual Message to Congress, January 16, 1981, jimmycarterlibrary.gov/assets/documents/speeches/su81/jec.phtml.

Congressional Research Service. "African American Members of the United States Congress: 1870–2012." Congressional Research Service Report for Congress, November 26, 2012.

"The Crusade for the King Holiday: The Protracted Efforts that Led to Holiday Bill's Passage." *Ebony* (January 1986): 36–38.

Evans, Freda, ed. "H.R. 3345—Martin Luther King, Jr. Legal Public Holiday." *Congressional Black Caucus Legislative Weekly 98th Congress,* August 1, 1983, www.avoiceonline.org/assets/txu-gwc-84-98-f8-01-1-1024.

Ferdman, Roberto. "What the Confederate Flag Really Means to America Today, According to a Race Historian." *Washington Post,* June 19, 2015, www.washingtonpost.com/news/wonk/wp/2015/06/19/what-the-confederate-flag-really-means-to-america-today-according-to-a-race-historian.

Freeman, Roland. *The Mule Train: A Journey of Hope Remembered.* Nashville: Rutledge Hill, 1998.

Gray, L. Lasimba, Jr. "If Beale Street Could Talk, It Would Tell Memphis to 'Copyright Me.'" *Tri-State Defender,* January 25, 2019, tri-statedefender.com/if-beale-street-could-talk-it-would-tell-memphis-to-copyright-me/01/25.

Harris, Aisha. "Stevie Wonder Wrote the Black 'Happy Birthday' Song … for Martin Luther King!" *Slate,* December 20, 2016, slate.com/culture/2016/12/stevie-wonder-wrote-the-black-happy-birthday-song.

History, Art, and Archives. "Hall, Katie Beatrice." U.S. House of Representatives, history.house.gov/People/Detail/14359.

Honey, Michael. "Memphis Sanitation Strike." Tennessee Encyclopedia, last updated March 1, 2018, tennesseeencyclopedia.net/entries/memphis-sanitation-strike.

Hoskins, Lotte, ed. *I Have a Dream: The Quotations of Martin Luther King, Jr.* New York: Grosset and Dunlap, 1968.

"How the Martin Luther King Jr. Birthday Became a Holiday." *Constitution Daily* (blog), National Constitution Center, constitutioncenter.org/blog/how-martin-luther-king-jr-s-birthday-became-a-holiday-3#.

Israel, Josh. "The Ferocious Fight Against the MLK National Holiday." Think Progress, January 19, 2015, archive.thinkprogress.org/the-ferocious-fight-against-the-mlk-national-holiday-cc5debdbb86a.

King Encyclopedia. "'I've Been to the Mountaintop.'" Martin Luther King, Jr. Research and Education Institute, Stanford University, kinginstitute.stanford.edu/encyclopedia/ive-been-mountaintop. Accessed July 6, 2020.

———. "King National Holiday." Martin Luther King, Jr. Research and Education Institute, Stanford University, kinginstitute.stanford.edu/encyclopedia/king-national-holiday. Accessed July 6, 2020.

———. "Memphis Sanitation Workers Strike 1968." Martin Luther King, Jr. Research and Education Institute, Stanford University, kinginstitute.stanford.edu/encyclopedia/memphis-sanitation-workers-strike. Accessed July 6, 2020.

"The Reverend James M. Lawson, Jr." Martin Luther King, Jr. Research and Education Institute, Stanford University, kinginstitute.standford.edu/encyclopedia/reverend-james-m-lawson-j. Accessed July 26, 2020.

"King Holiday." *Buffalo Challenger*, October 26, 1983.

Lackey, Hilliard. *Marks, Martin and the Mule Train*. Bloomington, IN: Xlibris, 2014.

Mullane, Deirdre, ed. *Words to Make My Dream Children Live: A Book of African American Quotations*. New York: Doubleday, 1995.

Odell, Robert, Jr. "Beale Street, Violence, and the 1968 Sanitation Workers Strike." Owlcation.com, last updated May 11, 2020, owlcation.com/humanities/What-Happened-In-Memphis-After-Kings-Death-In-1968.

Peck, Ira. *The Life and Words of Martin Luther King, Jr.* York, PA: Scholastic, 1968.

Pink Palace Museum. "Cotton Carnival and Cotton Makers Jubilee." Memphis Museums, www.memphismuseums.org/pink-palace-museum/exhibits/the-mansion/cotton-carnival--cotton-makers-jubilee. Accessed July 6, 2020.

"Proceedings and Debate of the 90th Congress, Second Session." *Congressional Record* (March 28–April 9, 1968): 9227.

Proposal for Martin Luther King, Jr. National Holiday: Hearing Before the Subcommittee on Post Office and Civil Service, 97th Congress (1982).

Rayner, Brenda. "The First Black Faculty Member at Memphis State University Receives the Coveted Carter G. Woodson Award of Merit." Southwest Tennessee Community College, press release, February 12, 2015, www.southwest.tn.edu/events/press-releases/2015/Feb12.htm.

"Riding the Freedom Train." National Museum of African American History and Culture, Smithsonian Institution, nmaahc.si.edu/blog-post/riding-freedom-train. Accessed July 6, 2020.

Roberts, Steven. "King Holiday Bill Faces a Filibuster." *New York Times,* October 4, 1983, www.nytimes.com/1983/10/04/us/king-holiday-bill-faces-a-filibuster.html.

Romero, Frances. "Martin Luther King Jr. Day." *Time,* January 18, 2010, content.time.com/time/nation/article/0,8599,1872501,00.html.

Rothman, Lily. "What Martin Luther King Jr. Really Thought About Riots." *Time,* April 28, 2015, time.com/3838515/baltimore-riots-language-unheard-quote.

Santini, Maureen. "Reagan Hails King, Signs Holiday Bill." *Buffalo News,* November 2, 1983.

Scott-Heron, Gil. *The Last Holiday: A Memoir.* New York: Grove, 2012.

"Should Martin Luther King Jr.'s Birthday Be a National Holiday." Debate. org, www.debate.org/opinions/should-martin-luther-king-jr-s-birthday-be-a-national-holiday, accessed July 6, 2020.

Stang, Alan. "Martin Luther King, Jr.—Communist Fraud." Rense.com, January 6, 2004, rense.com/general48/fraud.htm.

Venson, R. Q., and Ethyl H. Venson. Cotton Makers' Jubilee Collection. Memphis and Shelby County Room, Digital Archive of Memphis Public Library, memphislibrary.contentdm.oclc.org/digital/collection/p13039coll1/id/39.

Weathersbee, Tonyaa. "How Martin Luther King Jr. Helped Memphis Sanitation Workers Fight for Dignity." *Commercial Appeal,* March 30, 2018.

Whitt, Wayne. "Widow Leads March Honoring Dead Husband." *Nashville Tennessean,* April 8, 1968.

Williams, Chris. "Stevie Wonder and Gil Scott-Heron's Fight for MLK Day." WaxPoetics.com, www.waxpoetics.com/blog/features/articles/stevie-wonder-and-gil-scott-herons-fight-for-mlk.

Withers, Ernest. "Reports on MLK's March 18, 1968, Visit." National Archives and Records Administration, archive.org/details/624575-on-mlks-march-18-1968-visit. Ernest Withers was a well-known and highly respected photographer in Memphis, Tennessee. He was an FBI informant who passed on information to the FBI about Dr. King and his staff regarding the sanitation strike, planned marches, business boycotts—all of their moves and actions.

Wolfenberger, Don. "The Martin Luther King Jr. Holiday: The Struggle in Congress, an Introductory Essay for the Seminar on the Martin Luther King, Jr. Holiday: How Did It Happen?" Woodrow Wilson International Scholars, January 14, 2008, www.wilsoncenter.org/sites/default/files/media/documents/event/King%20Holiday-essay-drw.pdf.

PHOTO CREDITS

1968
Author's personal collection (p. 1)

February 12, 1968
Glenda Robinson Oates Personal Collection (p. 7)

March 18, 1968
Library of Congress; National Archives and Records Administration (p. 13)

March 28, 1968
University of Memphis Libraries; Courtesy of Special Collections Department (p. 18)

April 3, 1968
University of Memphis Libraries; Courtesy of Special Collections Department (p. 24)

In the Meantime
Martin Luther King, Jr., Research and Education Institute at Stanford (p. 38)
Author's personal collection (p. 41)

May 2, 1968
Author's personal collection (p. 44)

My Life Was Full
Author's personal collection (p. 62)

January 15, 1981
Author's personal collection (p. 64)
Author's personal collection (p. 65)
Author's personal collection (p. 68)

The Silver Lining
Author's personal collection (p. 72)

Stevie Toured On
Author's personal collection (p. 73)

1983
Author's personal collection (p. 77–78)

October 19, 1983
Collection US House of Representatives (p. 82)
Courtesy of Ronald Reagan Presidential Library (p. 83)

Backmatter
All photos from the author's personal collection (pp. 88–90)